The End

From Spir ...ng
to
Apostolic Covering

With Special Information
on Armor Bearing in the
End-Time Church

By Apostle Pernell H. Hewing, Ph.D., Th.D.

From Spiritual Mentoring to Apostolic Covering

Dr. Pernell H. Hewing
Sanctuary Word Press
921 W. Main Street,
Whitewater, WI 53190-1706
Phone: (262) 473-7472
Fax: (262) 473-9724
Email: hewingph@idcnet.com
Website: www.thesanctuarywhitewater.com

This publication is a tool to teach, to train, and to inform Christians, and also to minister and lead Christians into a deep ministry of God's Word and Work.

Scripture quotations are from the King James Bible © 1908, 1917, 1929, 1934, 1957, 1964, and 1982 by the B.B. Kirkbride Bible Company, Inc.

For additional information,
contact *Sanctuary Word Press*, (262) 473-7472.

Printed in U S A
First Printing 2002
Second Printing 2007
Third Printing 2013

The End-Time Call For...

Spiritual Mentoring...

Teaching, Training...

Spiritual Fathering...

Spiritual Mothering

and

Apostolic Covering

By Pernell H. Hewing, Ph.D., Th.D.

"Unto thee, O LORD, do I lift up my soul.

"O my God, I trust in thee: let me not be ashamed, let not mine   enemies triumph over me.

"Yea, let none that wait on thee be ashamed: let them be ashamed which transgress without cause.

"Show me thy ways, O LORD; teach me thy paths.

"Lead me in thy truth, and teach me: for thou art the God of my salvation; on thee do I wait all the day. "

Psalms 25:1-5

Table of Contents

PART III: Apostolic Covering

"Now he that planteth and he that watereth are one: and every man shall receive his own reward according to his own labour.

"For we are labourers together with God: ye are God's husbandry, ye are God's building.

"According to the grace of God which is given unto me, as a wise masterbuilder, I have laid the foundation, and another buildeth thereon. But let every man take heed how he buildeth thereupon.

"For other foundation can no man lay that is laid, which is Jesus Christ."   I Corinthians 3:8-11

Preface

The following information is written for the Body of Christ because God is hearing the heart cry of His people for someone to come in close and lead and guide them in their spiritual journey. What they do not know is that God Himself orchestrates their heart cry. God knows the need for the Body of Christ to have someone come in close to help them fulfill their eternal purpose.

The Lord wants to use His choice servants as mentors, teachers, trainers, spiritual fathers/mothers, and Apostolic Fathers/Mothers to come in close to believers and impart to and sow spiritual knowledge into special ones called of God for a special purpose. The Lord needs true Apostles to oversee these Kingdom Ministers to prepare them for Kingdom Ministries.

Special Apostolic Covering is needed for God's work and God's special called out leaders who have launched that special work of the Lord. Many have been looking for that special one to come beside him/her, but so many of them do not know what they need or who they need, but they know they need someone. Also many do not know how to accept one who is willing to come in close to them and/or they do not know how to submit.

Little or no information is written about spiritual mentoring, spiritual fathering and mothering, and Apostolic fathering/mothering. A dearth of information is written about Armor Bearing, and many are armor bearing and believing that is their mentoring. Sometimes, however, an armor bearer receives little or no formal mentoring.

This treatise will include information on the pitfalls of armor bearing and how both in the relationship may come short of God's plan of mentoring.

This treatise explains the difference between the different assignments God gives his servants for another's life, i.e. **mentoring, teaching, training, spiritual parenting** which sometimes includes natural **re-parenting, armor bearing, Apostolic Covering,** etc. Many who read this may see that they are already doing what is written here. Perhaps this will help those who are called to **mentor** to put some definition to it and divine order to it so that the power of God will be upon what is being done.

Spiritual mentoring, teaching, training, Spiritual Fathering and Mothering, and armor bearing have been done over the years, but much of the power God sent forth was lost because it was done without divine order. Satan entered into the relationship and did not allow the persons involved to identify the relationship.

One may have stayed close to an anointed leader to glean from or to be like the leader, but did not establish a clear relationship of submission and obedience to receive the impartation in the Spirit. The leaders, too, may not have put definition to the relationship.

Many tried to receive impartation from an Apostolic leader, but because of some fleshly mindset did not allow themselves to be identified with that person or submit to that person because of either the person's race, gender, social status, education, etc. Perhaps that leader did not line up with what the protege wanted, or the protégé did not want others to know that he/she was a protégé of an individual who is not famous.

8

This information focuses on **spiritual mentoring, spiritual fathering, mothering, spiritual teaching** and **training,** all of which is needed for the Kingdom to come into the Church. Presently, God is calling forth **Apostolic Fathers and Apostolic Mothers** to come beside His choice called-out servants and to serve as **apostolic covering** to many of his special ministries. Apostolic father's or mother's assignment and apostolic covering differs in function and relationships but inextricably interwoven.

God has laid it on many hearts to come and ask someone to cover or mentor them in some way--God has put it in their hearts to ask that one, and some has accepted the assignment. Hopefully, this book will add definition to apostolic fathering, apostolic mothering and apostolic covering. Also, it is hoped that many will be willing to enter this uncharted waters for Kingdom ministers and ministries.

The information in this treatise is for anyone who God assigns to one of His choice servants called to this type of ministry. This information will help one to understand covenantal relationship, identify roles and understand commitment in covenantal relationship. This information is will help the reader to understand each role's responsibilities in the covenant relationship.

How this Book is Divided

This book is divided into three parts. **Part I** discusses Spiritual mentoring, spiritual training, spiritual teaching, Spiritual fathering/mothering, and Apostolic fathering/ mothering. This part will provide help not only to the one who is called to mentor, teach, train, and/or spiritually parent (which also involves some natural reparenting), but also information for the believer who needs the help.

Part II covers Armor Bearing in and for preparation for the ministry. Some churches identify this ministry as the ministry of helps, and some don't put a name on it. For practical purposes, it is identified in this book as *armor bearing*. This information on armor bearing may not be new, but it will help shed light on aspects of armor bearing badly needed in the Body of Christ.

Part III of the book includes information regarding apostolic covering and in relation to spiritual authority and spiritual covering of ministers and ministries. The success of what is suggested here is predicated on one's understanding of spiritual authority in and for the ministry. For a thorough study of spiritual authority, obtain a copy of the book, *Spiritual Authority*, by Pernell H. Hewing, Ordering information is included in the list of books at the end of this book.

Special note: Apostolic mothering is new for the Body of Christ, but it has always been there. A church family needs a mother as well as a father. Apostolic mothers are just coming to the forefront and being identified, because their gifting and calling has been released and because of the release of the Kingdom Apostolic/Prophetic Church.

Please read through this information carefully and choose to allow God to speak to you about this important topic. Be willing to come in close to a called out one who is identified in this treatise as a "protege" who needs help. If one reading this is the "protégé," be willing to submit to the one God sends to bring you to your eternal purpose.

Pernell H. Hewing, Author

PART I

Help Wanted: Apostolic Mentoring, Teaching, Training, Mothering, Fathering

*Leader
Protégé*

*Protégé
Leader*

God Directs the Relationship

God Leads the Apostolic Leader
God Leads the Protégé Through
the Leader

By Apostle Dr. Pernell H. Hewing

Definition

of
terms

Spiritual Apostolic Mentoring, Teaching, Training and Spiritual Fathering/Mothering, Apostolic Mothering/ Fathering, Apostolic Covering are the subject of this treatise. Although a shade–sometimes a fleeting shadow–of meaning exists for each, they may be referred to in this writing to mean the same thing. Most importantly, each represents a three-way covenantal relationship ministry which is established and maintained by God Himself.

The Apostolic mentor/leader is sent by God to do a special work–the work of preparing one for his/her eternal purpose. The Apostolic mentor/leader is in covenant with God for the assignment and in covenant with the protégé for the assignment.

The protégé is in covenant with God and with the Apostolic mentor/ leader God has assigned to come in close with the protégé to lead and guide him/her in his/her spiritual journey toward his/her eternal purpose. Conversely, the Apostolic leader does nothing but what God leads him/her to do, and the protégé trusts God and obeys as led.

Chapter 1

Spiritual Children are Crying Out
to the Lord for Help

"And this is the confidence that we have in him, that, if we ask any thing according to his will, he heareth us:

"And if we know that he hear us, whatsoever we ask, we know that we have the petitions that we desired of him."
I John 5:14-15

One receives the Lord by heartfelt confession of Jesus Christ as Lord and Savior; however, if one is to grow and mature in the Lord, that one needs someone to come alongside and minister to him/her. That one needs someone to love, teach, train and guide him/her with a spiritual eye and help that one his/her spiritual journey. Although that person may be a pastor of the convert, this treatise refers to a relationship that is an added dimension to pastoring.

Many know that they need someone to come in close to them to lead them in their spiritual journey, but many think they cannot find anyone who will take the time. Know that spiritual mentoring, teaching, training, mothering, fathering, leading is a God thing, not a flesh thing. Because it is a God thing, God is ready to send someone alongside to lead and guide.

It is written...

"Behold, the eye of the LORD is upon them that fear him, upon them that hope in his mercy;" Psalms 33:18

"I will instruct thee and teach thee in the way which thou shalt go: I will guide thee with mine eye." Psalms 32:8

The Spiritual MENTOR
Sometimes Wears Many Hats

The work of an Apostolic **mentor** and the role of a spiritual **mentor** is not clear cut. A spiritual **mentor** may often take on the role of **spiritual mother** or **father**, **apostolic leader, teacher, trainer,** and many others. However, a **mentor** may be one who comes beside one and leads and guides one through simple things which are necessary for spiritual growth.

A spiritual or Apostolic **mentor** may be a **teacher,** but each has distinguishing characteristics. A **teacher** loves information and is always ready to provide the **Protégé** with information. Because a **teacher** enjoys education and study to learn, he/she will always be ready to impart and teach new information. A **mentor,** on the other hand, loves the **Protégé** — the **teacher** loves the **protégé** also — enjoys imparting and studies to sow into the **Protégé's** life. A mentor/teacher, therefore, does it all.

14

Mentors are not necessarily cheerleaders. They are coaches. Their role is not merely to confirm what one is doing correctly. Their goal is to correct that one and prevent that one from making a mistake. Mentors may be assigned the role of spiritual father or spiritual mother, and will encourage and rejoice with the Protégé, but they are there to press one on to greatness. This is often done through coaching and correction—not codling and nursing that one.

The main distinguishing feature of the **apostolic mentor's** role is a willingness to come in close to the protégé. A

mentor loves the protégé, enjoys imparting, and loves to sow into the protégés life. The **mentor** may teach and train, but he/she loves to impart. Sometimes this is done through teaching, sometimes through training, but often just by being available to the protégé and spending time with the protégé. Again, the apostolic mentor may or may not be one's pastor.

It is written...

"...I will give you pastors according to mine heart, which shall feed you with knowledge and understanding." Jeremiah 3:15

15

The role of a **mentor** in one's life may be missed or taken for granted because the one God may have assigned has the time to spend with the protégé and does spend much time with the protégé. The mentor may be a parent--parents are assigned the role of mentor by God, a relative, or thought of as a friend. Because that one is in such close relationship with the protégé, the protégé may not respect that one as **mentor** and miss the purpose of the relationship and the spiritual blessing of the relationship.

If one does not value the **mentor's** relationship or recognize it as a spiritual relationship — which is difficult to do if it is a close relative or friend — God will not honor it and the spiritual impartation will fall on dead ground. If the protégé looks down upon the **mentor** in a condescending way, the work the **mentor** is assigned to do will be blocked.

Sometimes the protégé may be better educated than the **mentor**, or has a better life style, or the **mentor** is a minority or a female **mentor** assigned to a male of high social status or of the supposedly spiritual elite. The protégé may also see him/herself more gifted and know more spiritually than the **mentor**. When that happens, God withdraws the assignment of the **mentor** for that one.

Although the Bible says the eye of the Lord is upon them that fear Him, and that He would instruct and teach, He uses His servants to be the catalyst to carry out this assignment. Since God makes the assignment, He knows what servant He has who can fulfill the assignment, and He knows if one is ready to submit to what one needs. When God assigns His servant to a protégé, He calls the protégé to obey.

It is written...

"Be ye not as the horse, or as the mule, which have no understanding: whose mouth must be held in with bit and bridle, lest they come near unto thee."
Psalms 32:9

Different ones will come alongside a believer and come in close to a believer at different times, but the ones who come in will be sent by God to help that one come in closer to God's will and way in a particular aspect of life. These different ones will lead and guide sometimes in financial matters, family matters, in mothering, fathering, in relationships, ministry, etc.

Apostolic mentoring, teaching-training, is somewhat different from mentoring that occurs after one is born-again, which is mentoring, teaching, training to help one understand Christianity and to help one grow in the faith.

Apostolic mentoring is when God has sent and assigns a seasoned Apostolic saint to come in close to prepare a called out one— to prepare that one for a special work of the Kingdom.

As one surrenders his/her life to the Lord, the Lord will know what that one needs to lead and guide his/her spiritual journey. However, that one needs to know and be ready for the one needed. Before one can be ready, that one must be able to identify what he/she needs; therefore, the question one must seek an answer to is, "What is needed for one's eternal purpose journey?" One must know if he/she needs or wants a **mentor**, a **teacher**, a **mentor/teacher**, a **teacher/trainer**, a **spiritual mother**, a **spiritual father**, an **apostolic mother** or an **apostolic father**. The one called to a special called-out leader for guidance may not know what he/she needs, but will find out if the one seeking leadership is not rebellious, or stubborn, and if he/she has dealt with heart issues or is willing to deal with them.

Although one person may serve in a believer's life in one or in varied ways, one may fulfill only one role. The one sent to lead and the one that is being led must be able to identify the main spiritual role that one has been sent to fulfill for this spiritual journey. Both must know and accept his/her spiritual role and enter into that role as an assignment from God.

Different ones will come when the need is there, and sometimes exit that one's life when the role has been completed. This role may appear as though it is a parenting role, but it is spiritual parenting; therefore, it must be led and guided by the Lord Himself. It must be all spiritual as any fleshly aspect of the relationship is an abomination to the Lord. The one sent to lead must be sanctified unto the Lord in order to keep the relationship all spiritual.

THE SPIRIT OF OBEDIENCE is the ruling force in the relationship between the protege and an apostolic leader. The one the Lord has sent to do the leading must be ready to submit his/her life to the Lord in unconditional surrender. That one then will be able to submit to a godly **teacher/leader**, as God would lead. If one does not understand obedience, that one may have difficulty obeying God. That one will also have a difficulty obeying someone sent by God to lead him/her.

The following will provide some much-needed insight on the clarion call for this ministry at this time:

1. To uncover that often missing link in spiritual preparation so that the believer and the one sent by God to lead and guide a believer on his/her spiritual journey can guide that one into a deeper understanding of the ways of God.

2. To help the one who needs someone to come alongside to lead and guide, but cannot seem to find one.

3. To help one who needs a spiritual **mentor, trainer, leader** to identify his/her need because often what one wants is not what one needs.

4. To help one know how to recognize that one God has ordained to come in close to lead and guide into God's ways.

5. To understand the covenantal relationship which must be formed, and how to establish that commitment clearly.

6. To understand, respect, honor, and how to bless the one God has sent to lead you on your spiritual journey.

7. To help the believer and the apostolic leader not take anything in the relationship for granted, but to understand all that is done in that relationship is of the Lord and for the Lord.

8. To help each understand his/her role and serve in that role as led by the Lord.

Notes

Chapter 2

Identifying and Distinguishing Wants and Needs for Leader

The question one must ask is, "...is the want/need for a **mentor, teacher, trainer, spiritual mother, spiritual father, apostolic mother, or apostolic father?**" The greatest perceived need is for an apostolic father. However, one may soon discover that there is a dearth of apostolic fathers. Also those with the apostolic father's anointing are over worked. First, one must identify what he/she needs and/or what one wants to impact his/her life and for impartation for spiritual ministry. After identifying what one needs and wants, then one can seek a person who has the heart to meet that need.

God stands ready to assign what one needs, but the one he assigns can impact or impart only as the relationship is identified and accepted by both parties. Although, what one initially identifies as what he/she thinks the need is may not be what that one needs; however, God may assign someone to meet the perceived need, and other needs may evolve and be met as the relationship is established.

One must know that his/her **mentor/teacher/trainer, spiritual mother, spiritual father, apostolic mother, apostolic father** is someone God has placed close to him/her for that one's spiritual journey. That is the only way for one's journey to be the journey of the Lord's leading. One must know that one has been assigned to him/her by God to unlock that one's greatness and help that one fulfill his/her eternal purpose. One should, therefore, enter into this type of purposeful relationship with great reverence as though it is coming from God.

The danger in modern Christianity is that one may need a special one who God wants to assign, but the **Protégé** is trying to draw from that one without clarifying the relationship or recognizing that this is a spiritual relationship. Also, the one God has assigned has not established the relationship and may or may not know he/she is the one God has assigned to the protégé to unlock that one's greatness.

The **mentor/leader** is to be committed to God for the relationship as the Protégé is to be committed to God for the relationship. They are then to be committed to each other for the spiritual relationship assigned by God. For this to happen one must be healed and delivered and all the corrupt nature i.e. of pride, rebellion, stubbornness, disobedience, control, judgmentalism, distrust, unforgiveness, resentment, anger, bitterness, and fear must have been hauled to the cross. *See illustration on the following page.*.

Many pitfalls exist when one is ready for a leader to come alongside and come in close to lead a believer in his/her spiritual journey. The first and foremost is unconditional surrender to the Lord and then the annihilation of pride. As one humbly submits to the Lord, that one can accept and be grateful for whom the Lord sends to lead.

The believer may be expecting, wanting, and desiring no one but the pastor or some spiritual superstar. However, the Lord may have someone else with more time or one with the special anointing for that assignment. It is at this juncture in the journey that the believer's pride is tested, and it is here that the believer may fail in his/her ascent into greatness. It is not whom the believer wants to lead and guide, it is the one the Lord chooses which will open the way for that one to enter into his/her greatness.

22

TAP-ROOT BONDAGES

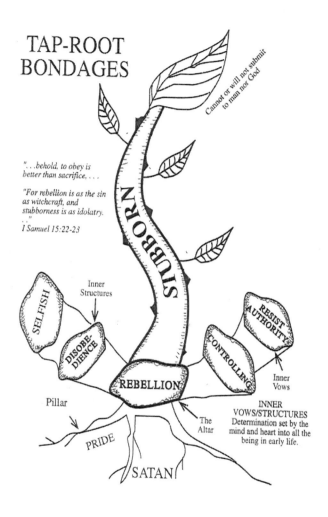

Cannot or will not submit to man nor God

"...behold, to obey is better than sacrifice, ...

"For rebellion is as the sin as witchcraft, and stubborness is as idolatry. "

I Samuel 15:22-23

STUBBORN

Inner Structures

SELFISH

DISOBE-DIENCE

REBELLION

RESIST AUTHORITY

CONTROLLING

Inner Vows

Pillar

PRIDE

The Altar

INNER VOWS/STRUCTURES
Determination set by the mind and heart into all the being in early life.

SATAN

Pride May Interfere with a Protégé's Accepting Whom God Sends

"Pride goeth before destruction, and an haughty spirit before a fall." Proverb 16:18

Because of pride, a **PROTÉGÉ** may not be open to receive anyone but the pastor or some spiritual icon. Both the Pastor and the ...Icon may be too busy with other assignments from the Lord to be available for the assignment to lead this believer on his/her spiritual journey. The Lord may also know that the believer is not ready for the kind of leadership the pastor or the apostolic leader is charged by God to do in a close relationship.

A pastor may be assigned by God to be a **mentor** or an apostolic leader to one, but generally his/her workload will not allow for him/her to be **mentor** and/or apostolic leader to many, especially to those with basic needs to prepare them for ministry. When God assigns him/her to one or a few, that means that pastor or apostolic leader must come in close to lead that one through the wilderness of the spiritual journey.

Some pastors have the time to be **mentors** to many. Some try to be spiritual **mentor** to every member in the congregation, and many do not understand the role of a close spiritual **mentor**. Many members, too many, on the other hand are waiting for the  pastor to be a spiritual **mentor** and/or spiritual mother/father when the pastor is not assigned to that task.

 STOP HERE

24

Allow God's Word to Minister to you.

Before you continue, read the following scriptures as follows: Hebrews 12:1-15; 22-29

Meet with the Lord three times in one week. Follow these procedures below each time you meet with the Lord.

1st reading: Read slowly pausing after reading of each verse.

2nd reading: Read the verse.
                Meditate on the verse, that is, read and
                then think on the verse.
                Read it again.
                Then pray the verse for yourself.
                If the Lord reveals anything, write it
                down.

Notes

Chapter 3

Mentoring, Teaching, Training, and Spiritual Parenting Interwoven

Mentor? Teacher? What is the Difference?

When a mentor is assigned by God to lead one and guide that one in his/her spiritual journey, the **mentor** will spend much time with the protégé and the protégé will try to take on the qualities of the mentor. Sometimes the leader has been assigned to be the protégé's **teacher**. If that one is merely a **teacher,** he/she teaches and hopes and prays that the protégé learns. However, the protégé must be willing to learn and choose to learn.

Spiritual Father/Mother? Mentor? Clarify role.

In the assigned role of **Spiritual father/mother** the **mentor** re-parents — sometimes in the natural things of life and then the spiritual things. They bring that parental love into the relationship that the protégé missed in childhood. The roles of a **mentor Spiritual father/mother** are somewhat different from an apostolic mother/father, although they may crisscross.

 Spiritual re-parenting is not clear-cut unless both the spiritual father/mother and the protégé are sold out to God for his divine purposes. However, this relationship is fraught with so many landmines. If the spiritual father/mother is not full of God's love and has any hint of the fleshly parent's love, the protégé will be short-changed. This is a holy relationship, a godly assignment, and if one loses sight of that, satan enters in and thwarts the divine purpose.

If the protégé is still hiding from life and love, has not been set free from the childhood Spirits of rebellion, stubbornness, rejection, control, and manipulation, that one will not grow an inch spiritually. That one may attempt to bring into the relationship all the childhood games played against natural parents, but since this is a God-assigned ministry, God will not allow the relationship to continue for the protégé.

One sent by God for spiritual fathering/mothering has been assigned an awesome task. This one needs a very close walk with God for this assignment and deep intercessory prayer training. The protégé, on the other hand, needs to be ready to pay the price of unconditional surrender to God and to the spiritual parent. The protégé must also have a deep, committed prayer life.

In order for God to allow one to continue with the assignment of mentoring/teaching and spiritual parenting one, the protégé must enter into the lessons. What God gives the mentor to teach, the protégé will need for his/her journey and God holds the mentor responsible to teach certain things, and God holds the protégé responsible to learn. The protégé must, however, have a teachable spirit and accept the teacher and the lesson as one assigned by God to impart this information to him/her.

Teacher! Trainer! Are roles the same?

An Apostolic leader may be a **teacher** and a **trainer** assigned to be a **teacher** and **trainer for the body of Christ.**

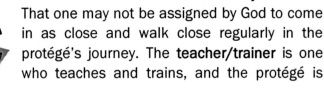

That one may not be assigned by God to come in as close and walk close regularly in the protégé's journey. The **teacher/trainer** is one who teaches and trains, and the protégé is accountable to show that he/she has learned by reproducing and allowing the **teacher/trainer** to check in some way to determine if the protégé did learn.

Why the need for a Spiritual Father/Mother?

If a **mentor** has been assigned to be a **spiritual father or mother,** that one has the awesome assignment of calling forth little boys and girls who are sometimes hiding in grownup bodies. In addition, the spiritual father/mother must minister love, acceptance, and guidance, while at the same time imparting spiritual knowledge and spiritual wisdom. One can see that this assignment requires that one be unconditionally surrendered to the Lord.

The **spiritual father/mother** must be keenly aware of his/her role, and that his/her role is assigned by God. The protégé must be keenly aware that this is God's assignment, and that it is all spiritual. Therefore, he/she must love, honor, and trust the spiritual father/mother. All fleshly expectations must be laid to rest on the altar, and all unholy reactions, which characterized relationship to natural parents, must be presented to the cross.

The **spiritual father/mother** must walk closely with the Lord and be sanctified enough to keep the relationship all spiritual. The Lord gives this one unusually deep love for the protégé, but that love must not have any hint of flesh attached to it. This one must, of necessity, prepare the protégé for a holy spiritual walk and spiritual living. Inordinate affections in the relationship leave the protégé open to compromise in holy living.

The **Spiritual father or Spiritual mother** may be a mentor, a teacher, a trainer, or a **teacher/trainer.** The assignment is clear in God's mind, and it should be clear to the one assigned as well as to the protégé. As both walk close to God, each will distinguish what the assignment is at a given time. Then and only then will God, Himself, be able to fulfill the spiritual purposes for which the assignment was made.

It is clear in my mind!

30

Chapter 4

Understanding the Assignment of an Apostolic Father/Mother

An **apostolic father/mother** assignment is deeper and broader than the mentor, teacher, or trainer--although the apostolic father/mother may mentor, teach, and train. The apostolic father/mother has an assignment from God to prepare the protégé for the protégé's eternal purposes and to try to make sure the protégé fulfills his/her spiritual destiny. The protégé must know that the following scripture applies to the relationship...

"Behold, I will send my messenger, and he shall prepare the way before me: and the Lord, whom ye seek, shall suddenly come to his temple, even the messenger of the covenant, whom ye delight in: behold, he shall come, saith the LORD of hosts." Malachi 3:1

When will God assign an apostolic father or apostolic mother? When the protégé has been called to a great work, but is not fully prepared spiritually and naturally to begin. One may have carved this call in his/her heart, but not know what to do with it. Sometimes one knows the call and is trying to begin the work with God's assigned apostolic direction. God, however, will recognize that one not only needs direction for the ministry, but some re-parenting.

The Apostolic Father/Mother is assigned by God because the protégé needs someone with great love, a love similar to a parent's love, to come in close and love, lead, guide, exhort, and encourage the protégé to bring that one's eternal purpose into focus, whether the protégé's work is in the embryonic stage or early beginning. The Apostolic Mother/Father will see it clearly as God sees it and try to bring it into focus so that it can be established.

The protégé may not be ready for the firm direction and close watch of an apostolic father/mother, and the protégé may not want God's assigned leader to come in close. The protégé may withdraw after he/she discovers that the apostolic leader's assignment by God will be to do a deeper work for which the protégé's very life will need be dismantled and rebuilt with Holy brick and mortar. The apostolic leader  is assigned to unlock the protégé's greatness; therefore, the **apostolic father/mother** is always aware of his/her responsibility to God and will do what is necessary to fulfill that responsibility.

When one is called to be an **apostolic father/mother,** that one has been tested and tried by the Lord and has not been found to be wanting of love and appreciation by the protégé. The **apostolic father/mother** has much unadulterated love to share, but is keenly aware that he/she has been given the awesome responsibility to prepare the protégé for his/her greatness.

It is written...

"...who may abide the day of his coming? and who shall stand when he appeareth? for he is like a refiner's fire, and like fullers' soap:

"And he shall sit as a refiner and purifier of silver: and he shall purify the sons of Levi, and purge them as gold and silver, that they may offer unto the LORD an offering in righteousness." Malachi 3:2-3

Because the **apostolic father/mother** has such great love and walks in such overt love, the protégé may be drawn to that love. It is because of the special anointing on the **apostolic father/mother**, which bespeaks of love, care and personal concern, that the protégé may be drawn to that one and wants that one to be his/her mentor.

The **apostolic father or mother** has passed through the corridors of mentoring, but will mentor if needed. That one is now assigned to do a deeper work and is about stripping the protégé of unholy things.

The **apostolic father or mother** is led by the Heavenly Father to do a quick work in the life of the protégé, which does not leave room for one to hesitate over surrender. As the **apostolic father/mother** comes in close to the protégé, the protégé will be led along the pathway of a cross life. A mentor, teacher, or trainer may give the protégé time to ponder and try to give up something. The **apostolic father/mother** will put his/her finger on that thing and steadfastly press in until it is given up.

The **apostolic father/mother** knows that God wants to do a quick work in the protégé's life, and that he/she is responsible to co-labor with God in getting that work done. That is why one should not reach out for an **apostolic father/ mother** if he/she is too immature in the spirit to be ready for an **apostolic father/mother.**

The protégé needs to be walking close to the Lord in order to recognize what he/she needs and to recognize the one God has sent. Sometimes the protégé is only ready for a **MENTOR** and that one may be already in his/her life. That one may be a friend, a neighbor, a parent, a grandparent, another relative etc. The relationship takes on spiritual significance, however, when both accept it as a spiritual mentoring relationship that God has ordained to help in that one's spiritual journey.

Just one more game...

Sometimes God wants to assign someone special to the protégé, but the protégé is still playing games with his/her spiritual life. Perhaps the Lord has assigned a mentor, a teacher, and/or a trainer, and the protégé has not taken advantage of what was given or has taken the one God assigned for granted; thereby, taking God for granted. It means that the protégé has not surrendered all to the Lord; therefore, the Lord is not going to assign His Apostolic Mother or Apostolic Father to one who is not ready to surrender all.

Apostolic Leaders are Assigned by God—
One Does Not Choose

"And I will give you pastors according to mine heart, which shall feed you with knowledge and understanding." Jeremiah 3:15

The **apostolic father/mother** is God's man or woman assigned to establish the protégé in God's purpose and plan for the protégé's life. The work that one does is for God — not because that one wants it. The Apostolic leader, therefore, is appointed and assigned, but often one is assigned to a protégé because God has led the protégé to cry out to him for someone.

The protégé must never assume that the one he/she has chosen has been released by God to be the one to unlock the protégé's greatness. If God gives someone to be an **Apostolic Leader,** the protégé should not take that one for granted nor assume that the **apostolic leader** has to do anything for the protégé or with the protégé. The **apostolic leader** is accountable to God.

To get the spiritual work completed in one's life, the work for which the Lord has assigned a leader, whether it be a mentor, teacher, trainer, teacher/trainer or **apostolic father/mother,** please adhere to the following. To get the most of a God-given leader:

1. The protégé should be sure that the one he/she wants to be his/her leader is the one God has given to lead that one in his/her spiritual journey.

2. The protégé should be sure he/she respects God's given leader and does not have some hidden critical judgment about the leader's appearance, education, social status, race, gender, etc.

3. The protégé must be aware of pitfalls that may mitigate God's power in the relationship. That one should not get caught up in pride because of the close access he/she has to the leader and forget that the protégé is there to gain spiritually. That one should not get too caught up in serving the mentor to allow self to be mentored.

4. The protégé should identify his/her position in his/her heart and to the leader. That one is with the leader to learn, not to teach the leader nor should the protégé think the leader needs the protégé's expertise.

5. If the protégé thinks he/she is equal with the leader, and is a minister with the leader, the protégé is either out of order or the two have not clearly identified their relationship. The mentor/teacher often knows instantly whether one discerns his/her worth.

6. The protégé must stop thinking that he/she knows more than the leader, and that the leader needs to know what the protege knows. That may be true, but if God sends A leader, that one can do what God wants.

7. Although the leader can do well without the protégé's help, the Lord will use the protégé's gifting for the leader's benefit. The protégé should keep the focus on what the leader can do for him/her and let God tell him/her what to do for the leader — and he/she will do much for the leader.

8. The protégé should not try to impress the leader, try to receive from the leader. The protégé should not ask the mentor to celebrate what God is doing in the protégé's life, rather draw from the mentor/leader's.

9. The protégé should not take access to his/her leader lightly. He/she may not always be there, so draw deeply from the leader's well now while one has access. This is especially true for armor bearers. Any time spent with the leader is time for mentoring, teaching, training, and impartation.

10. The protégé should not use time with his/her leader as fun time or regular friendship. The protege may have good times with the leader, but it is God's time. The protégé should use every minute as time God has provided something special that the protégé will need.

11. When the leader begins to be thought of as a friend, sister or brother, spiritual impartation stops with that identification. For example, when the protégé thinks of his/her leader as friend, it strips the leader of that one mantle in which is the protégé's help. The protege may want to reduce the relationship of mentor/leader to that of friendship so that the protege can be comfortable with the relationship, but when that happens, the protégé has touched God's anointing with the arm of flesh.

12. The protégé should treasure any invitation to be alone with his/her mentor/teacher. The protégé should not waste the leader's time or the time he/she has been given. The protégé should prepare to stay focused.

13. The protégé must be sensitive to his/her leader's need for quiet, rest, and for bodily needs. If one is an armor bearer or someone that is allowed close private time with the leader, he/she must not ask for attention before or after the leader ministers.

14. The protégé should avoid asking for personal counseling or sharing personal needs when the leader needs to prepare or is about to prepare for ministry — To do so touches the anointing. Also learn when it is not time for personal conversation. The protégé can let the leader know when he/she has a special need. The protégé should not pretend not to need help—choose the time.

15. The protégé's flattering words are not necessary. Persuasive words do not matter. The leader knows whether the protégé respects him/her.

16. Prayer is a key to a good, special relationship with the one the Lord has provided to bring forth ones eternal purpose. The protégé should pray for his/her mentor leader, and pray and ask God how he/she can bless the one God has given him/her. Perhaps that one can do something to save the leader's time. The time given the protégé takes away from something the leader may need to do—give that time back in some way.

17. Consider sowing a sacrificial financial seed into your leader's life on a regular basis. Sometimes that seed can be used to pay someone to do something the leader left undone because of time, prayer and other attention given the protégé.

18. The protégé should commit self to God first, and know that the mentor/leader is God's provision for him/her.

19. The protégé should love, respect, and honor a mentor, but do not idolize that one. God is the only one to be exalted.

20. OBEDIENCE TO WHAT THE LEADER SAYS IS TO THE PROTÉGÉ IS IMPORTANT.

21. The protégé's commitment, respect, and honor of a mentor/teacher or an apostolic leader leads one to trust that leader and trust that God is leading that one, because God has given that one to the protégé for his/her spiritual journey.

22. The protégé's disciplined, consistent prayer life is key to avoid pitfalls. That one does need to pray and get confirmation from God so that when the leader tells him/her something, God is saying this for his/her life.

23. One should not ask one to be his/her mentor/leader if one does not want to obey or even consider what that one tells the protégé.

24. If one has not done what his/her leader said, that one should not expect that God will give that one anything else until he/she is obedient to what that one already knows.

Notes

PART II

The Ministry
of
Armor Bearing

Ministry for the

Armor Bearer

and

Ministry to the

Armor Bearer

"Let nothing be done through strife or vainglory; but in lowliness of mind let each esteem other better than themselves.

"Look not every man on his own things, but every man also on the things of others.

"Let this mind be in you, which was also in Christ Jesus:" Philippians 2:3-5

Chapter 5

The Ministry of Armor Bearing

"And David came to Saul, and stood before him: and he loved him greatly; and he became his armourbearer.

"And Saul sent to Jesse, saying, Let David, I pray thee, stand before me; for he hath found favour in my sight.

"And it came to pass, when the evil spirit from God was upon Saul, that David took an harp, and played with his hand: so Saul was refreshed, and was well, and the evil spirit departed from him."
I Samuel 16:21-23

The ministry of armor bearing is as illusive as the meaning of the words themselves when one tries to fit them into the role of armor bearer in the Body of Christ. There is no apparent definition one can look to for deciding the description of the ministry (the job itself) in the body of Christ; therefore, it appears that the role of armor bearer takes on the definition of what the persons involved in the relationship make it to be.

Even as one searches Webster's dictionary for the meaning of the words, one finds the meaning illusive. According to Webster, 'armor' is a defensive covering, protective covering as used in combat. 'Bearing' or 'to bear' means to support, shield, buckler. Putting those two words together one might identify an armor bearer as one who serves a leader as a protective covering, a support, a shield, a buckler.

43

This is a pretty good definition for armor bearing as to what that one is suppose to do. So often one thinks of an armor bearer as a servant or one who serves the leader, and that is true. A further search for the meaning of the word reveals that it means *"porter"*. A porter is a baggage man, a water bearer, water boy, caddie, shield bearer, conveyor.

If one follows the meanings attached to armor and bearer and tries to identify what an armor bearer does for a leader, it appears that most think of the position as one who carries the leader's bag, brings water, serves as a caddie, a water-bearer and a carrier, a messenger. That is why in some ministries and churches the role is referred to as "The ministry of helps."

Too often lost in the description of the job is the meaning, shield, protective covering, and buckler. Lost to the leader also is the truth that this is a ministry — a ministry for the leader to fulfill for the Lord, and a ministry to the armor bearer assigned by God himself. This ministry criss-crosses mentoring, training, teaching, spiritual fathering and spiritual mothering.

The general purpose of this treatise is to focus attention on the ministry of armor bearing as it is being done in the New Testament church presently. The specific purpose is to identify clearly the role of the leader and of the armor bearer, and to take a critical look at the problems and pitfalls of the ministry of armor bearing.

It is important that the believers involved in armor bearing understand that armor bearing is a ministry. The armor bearer is to be prepared by the leader for greater

Kingdom work, and the leader receives his/her assignment from God. That makes armor bearing a God-assigned ministry. It is an assignment of servanthood on the part of the armor bearer, and of giving of oneself as Jesus did. Jesus said of Himself...

> *"Even as the Son of man came not to be minis-tered unto, but* to minister, and to give his life a ransom for many. " Matthew 20:28

The Bible is not silent on armor bearing although the words 'armor bearing' are not mentioned in the New Testament. 'Armor bearing' is a service ministry, and the words servant, serve, and service are either mentioned or revealed in many passages of scripture in the New Testament.

The Old Testament gives broader meaning to the subject of armor bearing. Cursory reading of the Old Testament accounts of the acts of armor bearing may lead one to think of the armor bearer as one who carried the arms, the gear of the leader he served.

It is important to note that armor, according to the dictionary, is a defensive covering, a shield, a buckler, and most of the mention of armor bearer in the Old Testament refers to the leader of the armor bearer being in battle. Closer attention to the Old Testament accounts of the armor bearer reveals more.

As one seeks the Holy Ghost for his revelation of Old Testament accounts of the armor bearer, one sees that the armor bearer is carrying the leader's armor. One will notice also that the armor bearer trusts the leader and will follow where he leads.

It is written...

"And Jonathan said to the young man that bare his armour, Come, and let us go over unto the garrison of these uncircumcised: it may be that the LORD will work for us: for there is no restraint to the LORD to save by many or by few.

"And his armourbearer said unto him, Do all that is in thine heart: turn thee; behold, I am with thee according to thy heart." I Samuel 14:6-7

One also sees that the armor bearer fights with the leader and fights for the leader. It is written...

"And the men of the garrison answered Jonathan and his armour bearer, and said, Come up to us, and we will show you a thing. And Jonathan said unto his armourbearer, Come up after me: for the LORD hath delivered them into the hand of Israel.

"And Jonathan climbed up upon his hands and upon his feet, and his armourbearer after him: and they fell before Jonathan; and his armour bearer slew after him.

"And that first slaughter, which Jonathan and his armourbearer made, was about twenty men, within as it were an half acre of land, which a yoke of oxen might plow." I Samuel 14:12-14

46

The Old Testament accounts of the armor bearer reveals also that the armor bearer was loyal to the leader, but fearful unto death if he did not obey.

It is written...

"Then said Saul unto his armourbearer, Draw thy sword, and thrust me through therewith; lest these uncircumcised come and thrust me through, and abuse me. But his armour bearer would not; for he was sore afraid. Therefore Saul took a sword, and fell upon it.

"And when his armourbearer saw that Saul was dead, he fell likewise upon his sword, and died with him.

"So Saul died, and his three sons, and his armour-bearer, and all his men, that same day together."
I Samuel 31:4-6

One catches another glimpse of the power of armor bearing and how God chose armor bearers in the relationship between Elijah and Elisha. Evidence in this case points to the fact that the purpose of the relationship is to receive the mantle or to receive something from the mantle of the leader. Also revealed in the biblical account of Elisha and Elijah's relationship is why God chose a particular one to assign to a leader. It is written of Elisha and Elijah's encounter ...

"So he departed thence, and found Elisha the son of Shaphat, who was plowing with twelve yoke of oxen before him, and he with the twelfth: and Elijah passed by him, and cast his mantle upon him.

"And he left the oxen, and ran after Elijah, and said, Let me, I pray thee, kiss my father and my mother, and then I will follow thee. And he said unto him, Go back again: for what have I done to thee?"
I Kings 19:19-20

Of particular notice in this encounter with Elijah is that Elijah choose someone who was busy working in a capacity that suggested that Elisha was one who would serve well. Elisha's eagerness and willingness to follow revealed his character. A further revelation of his character was revealed when he noted that he wanted to pay respect to his father and mother. Another indication of his servant spirit is what he did when he went back to his mother and father. It is written...

"And he returned back from him, and took a yoke of oxen, and slew them, and boiled their flesh with the instruments of the oxen, and gave unto the people, and they did eat. Then he arose, and went after Elijah, and ministered unto him." I Kings 19:21

Note that Elisha immediately ministered to Elijah, that means he served him and took care of Elijah's personal needs. As one follows the relationship between Elijah and Elisha, one sees the faithfulness of Elisha to His assigned leader. It is written...

"And it came to pass, when the LORD would take up Elijah into heaven by a whirlwind, that Elijah went with Elisha from Gilgal.

"And Elijah said unto Elisha, Tarry here, I pray thee; for the LORD hath sent me to Bethel. And Elisha said unto him, As the LORD liveth, and as thy soul liveth I will not leave thee. So they went down to Bethel."
II King 2:1-2

Perhaps if the leader and the armor bearer could discern God's divine purpose of the assignment, both may approach it differently. Elijah knew the purpose of his assignment. He said...

"And it came to pass, when they were gone over, that Elijah said unto Elisha, Ask what I shall do for thee, before I be taken away from thee. And Elisha said, I pray thee, let a double portion of thy spirit be upon me.

"And he said, Thou hast asked a hard thing: nevertheless, if thou see me when I am taken from thee, it shall be so unto thee; but if not, it shall not be so." II King 2:9-10

As one studies Old Testament accounts on armor bearing, one finds servanthood, one finds undying loyalty, and one finds sincere trust of the leader. One will also discern—in the case of Elisha and Elijah—that it opens the way for the armor bearer to receive the leader's mantle. Where does ministry to the armor bearer fit into the relationship?

God orchestrates the ministry to and for the armor bearer. Sometimes the armor bearer receives his/her ministry just by being with the leader, and sometimes the leader will spend time just ministering to the armor bearer. It is necessary, however, for the armor bearer to be mature and have a strong prayer life so that he/she will not be in need of constant ministry.

Notes

Chapter 6

Problems Facing the Leader and the Armor Bearer

Many problems are involved in this glorious ministry of armor bearing where two people come together for this wonderful servant/master role and neither can define the role nor know what to expect. The two, therefore, make up the rules of the ministry as they go along. The ministry of armor bearing then becomes what the leader thinks or wants and sometimes what the armor bearer thinks it should be.

Sometimes the leader is completely unfamiliar with the purpose for which God provided him/her with a faithful servant. The leader may have no idea that this is a God thing provided for a divine purpose—the purpose of spiritual mentoring, teaching, training, and for ministry. The armor bearer on the other hand may just want to get close to the leader to be identify with that one who is in the limelight.

The armor bearer may not know that he/she has been assigned to this special leader because the armor bearer is one whom God has designated as someone destined for spiritual greatness in God's Kingdom. Since armor bearing is a God thing, the armor bearer needs to know that God has chosen his choice servant to be the one to unlock the armor bearer's greatness.

Armor Bearing is Fraught with Problems

Because armor bearing is such an important ministry, but so difficult to understand, it is important for each to know the purpose of the ministry of armor bearing and to identify each other's expectation. Before each can identify his/her expectation, or even if they can identify expectations, each must be able to work through the multitude of problems inextricably interwoven into armor bearing.

One problem should not be overlooked. Often an armor bearer is not assigned by God to serve a particular leader. The assignment may be a self-appointed assignment or an assignment appointed by the leader because of some fleshly reason.

Be not surprised that many armor bearers and leaders are together because of some fleshly reason. The armor bearer might be in position because of wanting to be seen with a particular leader. The leader may just want a particular armor bearer because that one is a hard worker and is willing to serve.

One may ask that if one is in the armor bearer position because of some fleshly reason, will God be able to fulfill the purpose of armor bearing. That purpose is to lead one to his/her eternal purpose such as was with Joshua and Moses. Joshua was Moses' minister—Moses' armor bearer. It is written...

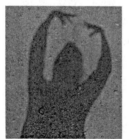

"And Moses rose up and his minister Joshua: and Moses went up into the mount of God." Exodus 24:13

Because the armor bearer's role dictates that he/she is not in the forefront, but stands behind and in the shadow of the leader, little is mentioned of Joshua until it was time for him to step into his eternal purpose.

It is written...

"Now after the death of Moses the servant of the LORD it came to pass,. That the LORD spake to Joshua the son of Nun, Moses' minister, saying,

"Moses my servant is dead; now therefore arise, go over this Jordan, thou, and all this people, unto the land which I do give to them, even to the children of Israel." Joshua 1:1-2

One can see that armor bearing has the divine purpose of preparing the armor bearer for his/her role of leadership. Because there is not a clear-cut method of training for that position, and because the armor bearer is so close to the leader, the leader may or may not take time for the training. How does the armor bearer get his/her spiritual mentoring and is spiritual mentoring a part of this relationship? God will work it out between the leader and the armor bearer.

The Relationship Between Spiritual Mentoring and Armor Bearing

One must not lose sight of the fact that this book is about spiritual mentoring, teaching, training, Spiritual fathering/mothering, Apostolic fathering/mothering and apostolic covering. It is important to know that armor bearing fits into this treatise as a ministry.

A major problem arises in this ministry of armor bearing when the leader may not take time to minister to the armor bearer and/or the armor bearer may pretend he/she does not need ministry and try to receive his/her ministry subtly or slyly. Since this is a God-ordained assignment, strong intercession on the part of each for one another will avoid this problem.

A leader assigned by God, who may or may not have learned how to let one into his/her sphere of life, may have a problem fulfilling his/her ministry responsibility to the armor bearer. Also, that strong leader may not know how to allow someone to serve him/her, because that one may have always served him/herself without help. The armor bearer then may become frustrated because he/she is not given freedom to serve, but his/her spirit is ready to serve.

Oftentimes leaders are introduced to the ministry of armor bearing and given a special armor bearer because God is trying to teach that leader a valuable lesson. One may wonder why God would assign one who is not ready for an armor bearer to work with one whom He deems ready for the ministry of armor bearing. It is as it is written...

"Herein is love, not that we loved God, but that he loved us, and sent his Son to be the propitiation for our sins." I John 4:10

The armor bearer may be the problem because he/she will not allow the leader into his/her sphere. The leader may know the need for ministry to the armor bearer, but is not given freedom by the armor bearer to minister as needed.

54

Because the leader has a Godly love for the armor bearer, that leader will not be allowed by God to go beyond what the armor bearer allows.

In order that the armor bearer receives the mentoring, teaching and training, the leader must be sensitive to his/her role. The armor bearer must understand his/her role, and both identify needs and wants in order to come to an understanding of how mentoring, teaching, and training can take place. Even when each identify purpose, another subtle problem exists which may not be easily expressed—ministry to the armor bearer.

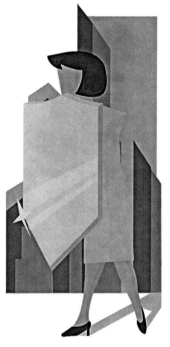

Often the armor bearer is crying out for ministry or is projecting him/herself into the leader's life expecting and subtly demanding ministry. This problem demands clarity as to how to meet the personal ministry needs of the armor bearer and when to meet those needs. Although there are no clear-cut rules or guidelines of how the armor bearer will obtain ministry, mentoring, training, etc. God will provide what is needed if a few guidelines are observed:

1. Each should be committed to God for the relationship. The leader then will be committed to pray and intercede for the armor bearer, and the Lord then will speak to the leader's heart of the armor bearer's need for ministry.

2. The armor bearer must be sold out to God and unconditionally surrendered to the leader and the position of armor bearing.

3. The armor bearer must have a disciplined, consistent prayer life, and that one's needs for ministry will be far less.

4. The armor bearer should be sensitive to the leader and know when to ask for ministry.

5. Finally, the armor bearer should not be afraid or too proud to ask for ministry.

PART III

Apostolic Covering

The Need for Apostolic Covering
and
The Perils of Not Being Under Apostolic Covering

"Let this mind be in you, which was also in Christ Jesus:

"Who, being in the form of God, thought it not robbery to be equal with God:

"But made himself of no reputation, and took upon him the form of a servant, and was made in the likeness of men:

"And being found in fashion as a man, he humbled himself, and became obedient unto death, even the death of the cross.

"Wherefore God also hath highly exalted him, and given him a name which is above every name:

"That at the name of Jesus every knee should bow, of things in heaven, and things in earth, and things under the earth;"
Philippians 2:5-10

"Now ye are the body of Christ, and members in particular.

"And God hath set some in the church, first apostles, secondarily prophets, thirdly teachers, after that miracles, then gifts of healings, helps, governments, diversities of tongues."I Corinthians 12:27-28

Chapter 7

Apostolic Covering of Called-Out End-Time Ministers and Ministries

The foregoing treatise on mentoring, teaching, training, and spiritual fathering/mothering is applicable to apostolic covering of ministries. However, it is hoped that when one reaches the spiritual plateau to begin a special work for the Lord, a work which needs apostolic covering, that one would have passed through the mentoring, teaching, training, and spiritual fathering/mothering. However, all of these may come to bear in apostolic covering.

Perhaps for clarity one may make a difference between apostolic fathering/mothering and apostolic covering of ministries. The apostolic fathering/mothering occurs when one has begun a work for the Lord, but still needs spiritual fathering and mothering. The Apostle then not only continues to help the minister grow in his/her walk with the Lord, but also continues to train that one in the way of the ministry.

Much of what an apostolic leader does as an apostolic father or apostolic mother involves mentoring, teaching, training, and parenting. However, the one that has begun a work needs more than that. That one now needs an Apostle to watch over and lead in the establishment of the Kingdom work that has been started. The apostle then has the duel responsibility of not only preparing the minister for the task, but also watching over the work to make sure it is established in the Spirit, by the Spirit and through the Spirit.

Apostolic fathering/mothering and apostolic covering are fraught with many problems. Some of the problems are-- not understanding spiritual authority in and for the ministry, not being able to submit to spiritual authority because of having not been set free of rebellion, and not understanding the ministry. These are critical problems now because of the transitional period in which the church is now and the ones assigned to carry the church through this transitional period.

As one searches the scriptures, one gleans a clear picture of leaders of ministries who are under authority. Christ's example as he walked on earth reveals His total submission to his father. David, the man after God's own heart is a portrait of one submitting to earthly authority. The present-day church, however, is grappling with the problem of **apostolic covering** of ministries and those under authority or who should be under authority.

The Church is in a transitional period such as the time when John the Baptist and Jesus the Messiah were ministering on the earth. Their ministries were closing out the Law and preparing for the Holy Spirit's reign. They made the way and made ready a people to usher in the Church Age. John the Baptist and Jesus the Messiah confronted different problems while they were ushering in a mighty change.

The present-day church is on the threshold of the move of God that will usher in the King, and God is pouring out His Spirit upon many. For this reason alone, it is important that all in the church understand the need for apostolic covering and have an understanding of *Spiritual Authority* in and for the ministry. It is for this reason one must have an understanding of the need for apostolic covering, and how submission to *apostolic covering* will move the transition into success.

At the forefront now of the awesome move of God is the *Saints Movement.* That is the move when the saints are being awakened and anointed to operate in all the gifts of the Spirit. God calls many into various ministries — unlikely ones are called to unlikely ministries. The ones called do not fit the normal ministry profile of leaders, and the church can only recognize them if they have a spiritual eye.

Many being called to leadership in the End-Time New Testament Church have no seminary degrees, many are female, and many come from backgrounds and life styles far removed from what leads to church leadership. However, many of these unlikely ones are destined to take the Church through the transitional period to prepare the way for the King to Return. Conversely, many know little or nothing about *apostolic covering* in and for the ministry.

This final move of God that is destined to close out the Age of the mortal church puts a new light on the response of the unlikely ones called to walking under authority. This new move in the church does not change God's direction for *apostolic covering* nor the need to be under apostolic authority.

The problem that arises regarding apostolic covering, however, is that rebellion rears its ugly head. Many being called have not been healed nor have had their corrupt natures cleansed, and they know little or nothing about submitting to *Spiritual Authority*.

It now becomes the task of God's *apostolic* leaders to cover, to train, to counsel this new breed of leaders. It is so important and necessary for the undisciplined one called who must submit to earthly *authority* to understand *Spiritual Authority* in and for the ministry. Much training is needed, some mentoring, and much studying and praying. All this requires much submission to authority and absolute submission to God Almighty.

Whenever God calls forth a ministry for His divine purpose, God ordains an earthly authority and gives that earthly authority power and authority in the heavenly to protect, lead, and counsel ones he/she is delegated to lead.

Prayer groups, churches, and para-ministries are springing up without proper guidance and proper relational covering. Whenever God calls forth a ministry for His divine purpose, God ordains an earthly authority and gives that earthly authority power and authority in the heavenly to protect, lead, and counsel the ones he/she is delegated to lead. The one who begins a spiritual work must follow God's order regardless and wait until God delegates a particular leader to watch over that one in the spiritual realm.

Because of the disorder and the lack of submission to *apostolic authority*, satan is bombarding many who are being called to begin a work for the Lord, and many are being led astray because God's hand is not on the work. God may have called the new leader, and the new leader may know the call and is able to minister. However, that one needs to understand and submit to *apostolic authority* before his/her work will have any effect in the spiritual realm, or ever survive the onslaught of satan.

A great dilemma emerges. Many of God's *delegated apostles* do not know how to train, lead, mentor, and guide the new ministers thrust into leadership. The established church itself is staggering under this new problem. It does not know what to do with these newborn leaders and often ignores them. The Bible, however, is the source of help to which they can turn.

A close examination of *Spiritual Authority* in the New Testament reveals that the different levels of authority existed. There is, of course, the local level of authority within the local church. In the local level pastors and elders are the *Spiritual Authority* delegated by God.

I have no idea how to train these

Beyond the local authority is the authority of the apostles who normally oversee the work of God within a particular sphere. In many instances Bishops are the ruling overseers. Much of this will still exist in the new move of God, and this is where the end-time apostles are being activated.

Notes

Chapter 8

Wherever authority exists, abuse of that authority will rear its ugly head. God, however, has called and established authority structures so that levels of authority exist and become accountable to higher authority. In the Body of Christ, pastors, ministers, elders, apostles, and leaders delegated by God are called to lead, watch over, and prepare the new breed of ministers. God calls these established leaders for this awesome task of watching over this new breed of minister.

Will you walk

The saints emerging into leadership must walk close to God to know in the Spirit who to look to for apostolic leadership and apostolic covering. The leaders called to lead must also walk close to God to know how to discern the true from the false, how to prepare them and train them for the task ahead.

The established apostle delegated by God to train His new recruits to the ministry must be able to look beyond what he/she knows, and thinks, and get to the very heart of God. They will be dealing with people who know not the ways of the church, and know not how to submit to anyone for leadership.

Many of the new breed of leaders come into their calling — and they are called by God — believing they know what to do. They are far from submissive. It takes great love and much prayer and intercession to fulfill God's calling to prepare these young recruits to lead the End-Time Church into Victory.

The leaders delegated by God to watch over the new breed of ministers have an awesome responsibility to God, and must be in total obedience to God. There can be no jealousy, no selfishness, and no desire to control or be worshipped. They must also not try to be popular and well liked. That one must build an army of leaders for the Lord and that army must not be weak.

The one delegated by God must know that many are called to leadership in the End-Time New Testament Church, but few are chosen. Many will start and fail, many will continue and not bring forth any fruit and will not be doing anything to fulfill the plan and purposes of God for this End-Time Church. These will soon disappear from the scene.

Many extremes will emerge in every level of leadership.

Many extremes will emerge in every level of leadership. There will be those who are seeking title, who have some grandiose ideas of power, respect, and prestige. There will be leaders who are immature, but think they are ready for great kingdom work. Some ambitious novices will emerge as well as leaders who are wrongly motivated. God knows what to do about them and with them. The one delegated to lead them must move with God with discernment as God works.

66

It is such a critical hour for the church at this time that if the Church is to arise, that the one called to leadership in the End-Time New Testament Church will try to deal with the extremes. Unless God gives His End-Time appointed and commissioned leader to deal with the extremes, that leader must leave it to God and continue to do what God leads him/her to do about the extremes.

God's called and delegated *apostolic* leader has one concern, that of bringing forth an army of trained leaders who understand *Spiritual Authority* and obey *Spirituality Authority*. The appointed and commissioned leader would have dealt with the old self with its self-importance, self-exaltation, self-promotion and self-preservation. One, therefore, has one goal, to work as God works. That requires absolute obedience to God.

The appointed *Apostolic Authority* will prepare God's called out men and women for God and not for him/herself and his/her ministry. Only as he/she stays in a position with God that God can tell him/her what to do, and he/she will do it, then God will do what He has to do to perfect the one who must learn how to submit to *Spiritual Authority*.

Problems of Walking Away
from Leadership

Some called to *end-time leadership* have been trained and brought up in the church, but without any understanding of the Body of Christ. The truth of Body Life is foreign to them.

Their greatest failure will be moving ahead of God, and moving out from under the apostolic covering. Because they have been in the church for years, they think they know what they need to know to begin their own work. They do not.

> A great failure will be moving ahead of God and moving out from under apostolic covering.

Many of the new breed of leaders do not know they need to submit to some authority delegated by God. These new leaders will now be called to lead in the End-Time New Testament Church, which is the church without spot or wrinkle for which the Lord is returning. They must learn the rudiments through understanding and submitting to *Spiritual Authority*. They must know the true meaning of the scripture...

> *"Now ye are the body of Christ, and members in particular."* I Corinthians 12:27

Many of the newly called end-time leaders must understand the calling of the Lord and realize the seriousness of the preparation for that CALL. That preparation can be done as one is trained in the church under a prepared pastor or leader. Some of these new ministers seriously look to some older leader for covering, but do not receive it. That pastor or leader, however, may not want the responsibility or may not be adequate. They may not even have a training program.

The one the new minister is looking to for leadership may not be the one God will delegate to lead that one. However, because that one needing leadership is in that church, or feels comfortable with that one, he/she may not consider looking elsewhere for training and/or Apostolic

Covering. That one needs to seek God so that God can direct him/her to The *Delegated Authority* God knows can prepare him/her for the calling.

A greater failure is not moving at all because of fear or some other fleshy reason.

Many sit under the covering of a particular leader, and that leader has not thought of training one for the ministry and has no thoughts that the one who needs training is looking to him for training. The new leader may be crying out for training but will not leave the church for his/her ministry.

If the one waiting for training does not receive the training, often that one will leave a church and begin a ministry or a work for the Lord without proper apostolic covering. However, the work may be short lived because of the lack of proper apostolic covering. If it continues, often what God had ordained for a special ministry remains impotent because of lack of proper submission to authority.

What God had ordained for a special ministry remains impotent because of lack of proper submission to authority.

Another serious problem that exists in regard to apostolic covering of a work for God is that one called to a work may believe he/she is being covered for that calling merely because he/she is in a particular church. *Apostolic covering is a serious matter.* It is a Spiritual covenant between God and the persons involved. That covenant is for more than a leader helping one get a ministry started. That work started is to fulfill an eternal purpose in the Kingdom of God.

If a pastor or elder with the local church does not send one out, and/or commit to the ministry of covering the person and the ministry, the person is uncovered, and satan knows it. That person may be afraid to look elsewhere for covering; therefore, the only option is consecrated prayer. Who God calls, He will find an adequate and correct covering.

The new end-time minister often times will leave from under the one God has delegated as authority over that one before the time God requires. Often that one will begin a work with no one watching over him/her. Sometimes, one will seek the counsel of friends or someone who does not have the authority in the spiritual realm to protect that one and his/her work.

When a ministry is uncovered this leaves the new minister prey for the enemy. That is why some ministry never 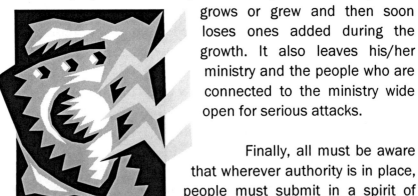 grows or grew and then soon loses ones added during the growth. It also leaves his/her ministry and the people who are connected to the ministry wide open for serious attacks.

Finally, all must be aware that wherever authority is in place, people must submit in a spirit of love. The one called now to the New Testament, End-Time Ministries must remain strong and submitted to God, yet totally open to the guidance and influence of the authority delegated by God.

.As the church moves forward, the lesson of *apostolic covering and submission to apostolic authority* must permeate the hearts and minds of the new breed of leaders and the ones called to serve as *apostles and leaders.*

This entire book is for both because each must understand mentoring, teaching, training, spiritual fathering/mothering, apostolic fathering/mothering, and *Spiritual Authority* in and for the ministry. They must understand the responsibility of and to each and to God, and they must be true intercessors.

Appendix

Epilogue

Notes from Practical Experience of the Writer's call to Help Unlock Spiritual Greatness!

The calling to be an Apostolic Covering, and sometimes a Spiritual mother sometimes an Apostolic Mother is very real to me. Before the assignment of Apostolic Mother was Spiritual mentor, teacher, and trainer. Having been anointed and appointed by God for this special work in the Body of Christ, I also obtained much spiritual training for Armour Bearing. I use the past tense, but am still somewhat engaged in every level of this training.

I had and still have ones the Lord assigns to me. I am committed to God for the ones assigned to me, to serve as mentor/teacher/trainer; however, My greater assignment is the assignment to be Apostolic Mother and an Apostolic Covering for Ministers and Ministries. God had assigned many to me, but now I am not as free to meet personally with the ones assigned to me, but I have in place ways to guide them on their spiritual journey.

The Lord has given me a special way to work with those God has chosen for me to come in close and lead, guide, and minister to while they walk on their spiritual journey. Much of it is teaching and training. I am not permitted to allow one assigned by God to me to stay where one is, nor am I to wait until one is ready to change. We move together toward change, and prayer and the Word of God daily will perfect this change.

I do not take one's word that he/she is entering into what I impart or teach. I will train in the Spirit, through the Spirit, and by the Spirit. The training will be done by bringing my beloved protégés into disciplined, consistent prayer and Bible study using the Word of God and material God has given me to prepare for this work. If one does not need training, that one does not need me to come alongside him/her.

God has given me many to bring forth into Spiritual greatness, and He has given me great love and care for each one. Because of the number of people the Lord has assigned to my hand, I don't have time for a friendly relationship. All my relationships are assigned by God, and we come into agreement as to the purposes of that relationship and our commitment to one another in that relationship.

 One may come to me with a strong calling, strong spiritual training and background. However, he/she will still need to enter into what He has given me to unlock their greatness for the Kingdom Church, They must be prepared for the End-Time Battle of the Age. The Lord hid me in the palm of His hands until I had written and prepared material for this time and for this training. This book is just one of the 58 books I have written for this purpose.

One may want to communicate regularly with anyone with whom God assigns as leader in a protégé's spiritual journey; however, because of the limit of time,, the number of people waiting for someone to come into their lives., time is limited to spend with a protégé. With that truth, one must be ready for complete submission to God so that one will not need so much personal attention. When one is in total submission to God, that one becomes easy to be mentored, trained, and covered. The apostolic call for the Kingdom Church requires endless hours of work. Therefore, an apostolic leader will not be available whenever a protégé wants — especially by telephone. As a matter of fact, one can help greatly if communication is by mail or fax or e-mail.

Finally, despite the perils and pitfalls of being an Apostolic leader, working with a protégé is a rewarding work. Being in covenant with God for the relationship draws leader and protégé into closer relationship with God. If a leader and a protege think they are ready for this type of relationship, ponder the questions on the following page before saying yes to the Lord.

"Now unto him that is able to do exceeding abundantly above all that we ask or think, according to the power that worketh in us,

"Unto him be glory in the church by Christ Jesus throughout all ages, world without end. Amen."
Ephesians 3:20-21

Pernell H. Hewing

Apostle of the Lord Jesus Christ

Appendix II
Questions for Thought and Prayer

1. Are you ready to grow deeper in the Lord through disciplined and consistent prayer and Bible Study?

2. Are you willing for the Lord to give you His choice of an apostolic leader?

3. Are you ready to make a deep commitment to the Lord to do what your apostolic leader assigns?

4. Are you ready to enter into a special covenant with the Lord and with your mentor/trainer (apostolic leader) to do what is assigned by your leader?

5. Will you allow the Lord to bring you into a consecration with Him which will be initiated by the Lord, Himself, after the true covenant is made?

6. Will you agree for the Lord's apostolic leader to watch over that covenant, and cover you in priestly prayers while you are going deeper in the Spirit to allow Him to finish the work in you?

7. Will you be accountable to your apostolic leader by keeping in touch as directed and following the directions given for this end-time preparation?

8. Are you ready to come away from the crowd, come in close to the Lord so that the Lord can teach you, train you, heal you, and deliver you from corrupt nature as your apostolic leader directs?

> *God wants you to live for Him and work for Him and to bring you into an intimate relationship with Him. Be sure you are ready to pay the price.*

Appendix III

Accountability

For each one who is ready for close, spiritual preparation for one's eternal purpose, be sure that your accountability to someone is not haphazard nor slip shod. Specific arrangements should be made to keep in touch with the one to whom you are accountable.

The one God assigned to a protégé should watch the protégé's progress, pray for the protégé, pray with him/her and be prepared to help that one in areas where he/she needs it. If faithful and consistent with his/her commitment, God will bless the relationship beyond what one can imagine.

If you are interested in this type of training, complete the following questionnaire and return the covenant, and the application for your mentor/teacher.

Covenant for Strategic Training and Mentoring/Teaching/Training

I, *(Protégé)* _____ ,

covenant with God and with_____ Mentor/Teacher/Trainer this _____day of _____20____, to enter into Spiritual Preparation for my eternal purpose.

I commit to developing and maintaining a disciplined and consistent prayer and Bible study life.

I will commit to a close relationship to follow through on my covenant, do what is assigned by my mentor/leader, and will maintain constant communication in the designated way agreed upon with my mentor/teacher/trainer.

Name

_____

Address

_____

State_____Zip_____Phone(_____) _____

****

I, *(Mentor/Teacher/Trainer)*_____

Covenant to pray for_____ and keep covered in prayer, identifying my role in and my expectations from the relationship; and review all material sent relevant to the agreed upon training as long as we both keep this covenant agreement as written.

Sign

_____Title_____

Date_____

Appendix IV

Part 1

Sample Questionnaire

Please take your time and complete this questionnaire. Pray much before you begin. The questions are to help your leader know you in the Spirit. Also, as you write and answer, the Holy Spirit will minister to you.

1. Name: _____ Date:_____

   Address: _____ Phone: (___)_____

   City/State: _____ Zip: _____

2. Age: _____ Marital Status: _____

3. Highest Educational Training: _____

   Occupation: _____

4.   Present Ministry Affiliation (Church, Pastor):

   _____

5.   If you don't mind, list as many former church

   affiliations as   you can remember:

   _____

   _____

6. Briefly explain your current ministry – in or out of your local

   church: _____

   _____

   _____

7. What do you think or know God has called you to do.
   Explain briefly: _____

   _____

   _____

   _____

8. How can I, your apostolic leader, help you? Explain: _

   _____

   _____

   _____

   _____

9. Briefly explain your prayer and word study: _____

   _____

   _____

   _____

   _____

Appendix IV, continued

Part 2

The following questions may require some writing, but pray and write from your heart on a separate piece of paper.

1. After pondering the nine questions on Appendix IV, Part 1, respond to all in a paragraph or two.

2. Write a page or two giving a profile of your beginning with your childhood joys, love, hopes, dreams, parents, hurts, disappointments, etc. Feel free to write what the Lord leads. Don't try to impress anyone. Write from your heart.

3. Briefly discuss your family relationships relationships, i.e., marriages, children, etc. Again, please don't try to impress, but write from your heart.

4. If you can, please write the complete vision that God has given you for your ministry.

83

The Ministry of the Mizpeh Covenant

This book focuses on the truth of the meaning of covenant-making and preparing for battle. It calls one to give up idols one must deal with. It then presents the truth of covenant-making from salvation to the covenant of grace to the purpose of covenant-making. A special feature of this book is an introduction to the cross life.

The New Sound of Zion

This is a photogenic view of End-Time Zion where the Lion of Judah resides. This book issues a call to every born-again believer in Jesus Christ to prepare for a new sound from heaven to open the way for the Lion of Judah to come. The New sound of Zion is a call to worshipers, dancers, musicians, and intercessors to choose to pay the price to release the New Sound whether it be song, dance, music or Intercession to open the way for the Lion of Judah to roar in the Church

The Hebron Ministry...A Ministry of Faith, Rest, and Refuge

This book leads one to and gives meaning to going wholehearted with God. The End-Time Believer enters into Faith and REST as God ordains. When one goes wholehearted with God, the Believer will find refuge with Him.

El Shaddai

The believer who enters into this ministry will receive new life, revival, restoration and "The Blessing". The believer will understand how much he/she is in need of a blessing, if that one missed out on the "Family Blessing" during childhood. This book also leads to the healing of the wounded spirit, awakening of the sleeping spirit, and release of the imprisoned spirit.

HEALING

The Healing Streams of Bethesda

This a call to a place of healing–a place to enter into the waters of life. The message of this book points one to the healer, Jesus Christ. A special focus is placed on the three keys of healing: the grace of faith, the grace of hope, and the grace of love.

Come to Gilgal for Circumcision of the Heart

This book is the treatise of the message in Joshua 1-6 relating it to the need for circumcision of the heart for a deeper walk with God. It deals with putting an end to wilderness wandering after salvation and entrance into a sure covenant with God for Intercession for the family. (CDs Available)

The Ministry of Jehovah Rapha with Concepts of Divine Healing

In Rapha one finds healing for deep wounds, emotional scars, debilitating illness and other traumas for which many have given up hope. The Lord comes unto us in Rapha to heal not only the body, but also heals the soul and spirit.

MINISTRY

Getting to Know the Holy Spirit and Preparing for Holy Ghost Baptism with Fire

This book is written for the purposes of pleading with the believer to seek for all what was promised and to be satisfied with nothing less than full power from on high. A special focus of this book is Baptism with Holy Ghost Pentecostal fire and preparation to work the works of God in power.

Practical Aspects of the Body of Christ and the Five-Fold Ministries for the Kingdom

A deep study of the Body of Christ and Five-Fold Ministry and the various aspects of the ministry with attention being given to the call and qualifications needed to move in the varied and different offices for End-time Ministries.

The End-Time Call for Spiritual Mentoring, Teaching, Training, Fathering, Mothering, to Apostolic Covering

This book explains the different assignments God gives His servants for another's life i.e. mentoring, teaching, training, spiritual parenting (which sometimes includes natural reparenting) to Apostolic covering. Also included is special information on armour bearing;

Shiloh El-Beth-el, Calling Believers in Christ... ...in Preparation for the Ministry of the Kingdom of Heaven

Shiloh El-Beth-el is representative of the Kingdom of Heaven – the Kingdom of God on earth. It brings into focus God's ways of dealing with mankind and how it establishes His plan and purpose for and with mankind. It takes one back to the first church in the wilderness and to the Levitical Ministry of the Old Testament.

Shammah, the Ministry of the Prophet/Intercessor and of God'sProphetic People

This is a book to help the believer understand the office of the prophet/prophetess, prophecy, and this end-time prophetic movement. The messages also focus on the life and calling of the Prophet Intercessor.

MINISTRY INTERCESSION

Spiritual Authority: Understanding and Submitting to Spiritual Authority Brings Power, Authority, and Anointing

This book presents a microscopic view of Spiritual Authority in and for the Ministry and the facets of Spiritual Authority often overlooked or not known by those who "*... walked not after the flesh but after the spirit.*" **Romans 8:4b.** This book helps one to understand how to enter into and walk in the authority of the believer and how to receive and walk in the anointing.

Repentance and Remission for Entrance into Kingdom Apostolic Work

This is a book of practical exercises to prepare one for the ultimate Kingdom ministry of remitting sins. The Purpose is to take the reader on a journey of forgiveness, Holy Ghost repentance, and remission of sins for one self. It is at the end of the journey that one is prepared for Kingdom ministry.

DELIVERANCE

Smashing the Influence of Tap-Root Bondages

This book focuses on smashing the influence of the tap-root bondages of pride, rejection, rebellion, stubbornness, disobedience, and fear. It is designed to prepare one for intercession by leading one into deeper revelations of these areas in their own lives in which Satan has them bound.

The Call to the Ministry of Deliverer Jesus Christ Jehovah-Sabaoth

The purpose of this book is to issue a call to the "called out" people of God to look together into the Word of God to find answers. The ministry of Sabaoth is for those who have come to the end of their strength and need deliverance—Jehovah-Sabaoth meet failure and offers deliverance.

PERSONAL GROWTH

In the Garden with the Risen Savior
This book is for anyone seeking a life centered in Christ or is already anchored in Christ. It reveals how close God can be to His own whether one trusts Him completely or whether one accepts His love, His kindness, His forgiveness.

Bring your Life to Divine Order
Through Two Forty-Day Consecrations
Presenting consecrations of fasting, travailing prayer, physical cleansing, and spiritual cleansing in preparation for unconditional surrender. This book presents guidelines for two 40-day consecrations for unconditional surrender. The first is a consecration of fasting, travailing prayer, cleaning, and putting the physical environment in order. The second is a consecration in prayer and the Word of God which leads to spiritual cleansing.

Into the Depths with Jesus
The writer captures the heart of God as she records His messages for the work of the Kingdom. An account of one person's journey with God, this book speaks to all who are seeking a deeper walk with God.

The Threefold Calvary Experiences of a Christian:
New Life, Death, and Resurrection in Christ.
This book is a call to look to Calvary for New Life in Jesus Christ. The information leads one through a Gethsemane Experience to death to self and into a Bond-slave Relationship with Jesus.

The Book of Ephesians

To get the Word of God in your heart, begin with the book of Ephesians. These are the study and ministry CDs and aid for memorizing scriptures. (CD only)

From Spiritual/Financial Insolvency to Financial/Spiritual Abundance

This is not a "how-to" book to read to glean more information about finances. It is a book to change your position in Christ. This can only happen as one completes Practical Exercises as directed.

FAMILY INTERCESSION

Calling Forth the Family (Priest) Intercessor
To Destroy Generational Line Curses

Guidelines for entering into a life of intercession and work of Intercession for the family. Information in this book introduces the the call to be *the Family (Priest) Intercessor* and what it takes to break the back of Satan and take family members out of his hands.

Understanding and Destroying the Power
in Generational Line Curses

This book is written is such a manner that one could learn enough to enter into the call to become **the Family (Priest) Intercessor.** As you grasp the information given here and say **'yes'** to what the Lord is saying, you will enter into a depth with Jesus where Satan will not be able to touch.

Divine Exchange of Curses for Blessings

This book gives an account of the battle to release the blessings in the family bloodline. It is the opposite of breaking curses, but the battle is just as fierce for unlocking blessings in the family bloodline.

Spiritual Journey into Intercession for Families in Desperate Situations

This book provides practical guidelines for interceding for a family member or for families in desperate situations. This book also calls the one praying into the position of Family (**Priest**) Intercessor.

Restoring the Beauty of Holy Matrimony

A manual of information for Married Couples, Couples Planning Marriage, Couples Planning Reconciliation after a period of Separation, and Couples contemplating divorce, or Couples locked into a troubled marriage, and for pastors, ministers and other marriage counselors.

THE TRIBES OF ISRAEL
The Tribe of Judah

This book provides a panoramic view of the Tribe of Judah beginning with his birth in Genesis and continues on into Revelations where the Lion as the Tribe of Judah comes on the scene. This gives a detailed account of Judah's ministry as worshiper, warrior, intercessor, king and priest in the End-time Church.

The Tribe of Simeon

This book provides an all encompassing view of the Tribe of Simeon commencing with his birth in Genesis and culminating in Revelations. This book gives a detailed account of Simeon's ministry as the Sword of the Lord in the End-time Church.

The Tribe of Benjamin

This book provides an all encompassing view of the Tribe of Benjamin commencing with his birth in Genesis and culminating in Revelations. This book gives a detailed account of the ministry of the End-Time Benjamites who come to the End-Time church preaching the Gospel with power.

The Tribe of Asher

This book provides an all microscopic review of the Tribe of Asher as presented in the Old Testament, and introduces the ministry of the End-time Tribe of Asherite in the Body of Christ as the one who has died to every desire except to engage in the ministry of Prayer, Intercession and warfare. The one who has the End-time ministry of Asher chooses to spend his/her life around the throne in the bridal chamber to receive the heart of the King for the Kingdom.

The Tribe of Manasseh

Manasseh is the son of Joseph adopted by Jacob as one of his own sons. The ministry of Manasseh is the key for the Kingdom as this is the ministry which will lift the church above the healing and wholeness to healing for the nations.

The Tribe of Ephraim

Ephraim is the second son of Joseph who was adopted by Jacob as one of his own. He is the one over which Jacob crossed his hand and gave him firstborn blessings although he was the second born. This book introduces the ministry of Ephraim for the Kingdom which is the one given to healing for the backsliding church.

The Tribe of Gad

The ministry of the End-time Tribe of Gad is deliverance of the church out of the hand of the enemy so that the church will be prepared for the Kingdom. This book provides the revelation that the higher purpose of the End-time Gadite ministry is to go beyond opening prison doors of the believers in Jesus Christ who are in need of deliverance, but also to deliver the church from the throes of satan and from satan's demonic infiltration.

The Tribe of Issachar

This book introduces Issachar as the Burden-bearer for the church. The End-Time Issacharite not only knows the times and seasons, but carries a ministry in for the Kingdom which encompasses one or all of the following: Intercessor, prophet, prophet intercessor, spiritual father, pastor, prayer warrior.

The Tribe of Zebulun

This book gives a historical account of the life and works of the Tribe of Zebulun in Israel and into the ministry for the Kingdom. The ministry of the End-Time Zebulunites is a Kingdom Evangelistic ministry. The Zebulun ministry will lift the church out of the four walls and open the way for a harvest to souls.

The Tribe of Dan

The ministry of the Danite in the Kingdom is multifaceted, but it begins and ends with a ministry of judgment. The Danite ministry will open the way for healing of the believer which is needed because of one missing the blessing of natural parents. The End-time Danite will be positioned in the church and the Kingdom to know and to see—especially see and discern unholy priest/pastor/leader in the Church

The Tribe Napthtali

The Ministry of the End-Time Napthali is Prophetic Intercessor, Watchman and warrior. Napthtali is a hind let loose: he giveth goodly words. The Ministry of the Naphtali in the Kingdom is the Prophet-Intercessor in the Kingdom who has been brought into a hidden place with the Lord in order to be the hind loosed to destroy the enemy camp in and over the church.

The Tribe of Reuben

Reuben is the first son of Jacob, but did not receive his firstborn birthright. The ministry of the End-Time Reubenite is to bring the church to see the Son, Jesus Christ. As the Reubenites come on the scene in the church, eyes will be opened to see the Son, high and lifted up, calling the church up higher to enter into the Kingdom.

The Tribe of Levi

This book will lead the reader along a pathway to unconditional surrender and to live as the priest of old in order to become End-Time ministers of the Kingdom. The ministry of the End-Time Levite is the ministry of the Royal Priesthood. The signs of the times are upon the Church for the End-Time Levitical Minstry to come forth and open the way for the King to come.

Order from:
Sanctuary Word Press,
921 W. Main St., Whitewater, WI 53190-1706
Phone: (262) 473-7472 † Fax: (262) 473-9724
E-mail: hewingph@idcnet.com
Website: www.thesanctuarywhitewater.com

A Glimpse of the *Sanctuary*
The place from which this book originates...
A Special Place for Christians
to Get Away.

The *Sanctuary* is a place where believers come for a time of refreshing in the presence of the Lord, and they enter into deeper depths with God. Each of the rooms in the *Sanctuary* used for overnight stay has a special ministry and persons coming for a time with the Lord hear the call to enter into that Ministry.

Readers of this book are encouraged to inquire about coming to the *Sanctuary*. However, God has given permission to release this book so that those who never come to the *Sanctuary* will hear the call and enter into their Ministry. One can do so by following the directions in this book.

† The *Sanctuary* is a peaceful and warmly decorated house that has approximately 25 rooms. Lodging is similar to a family-style "bed and breakfast" although meals are not served except for special occasions. The *Sanctuary* is a non-denominational and spirit-filled ministry retreat center. Bible classes, prayer and various other body ministry meetings are held regularly in the building.

	HOLY OF HOLIES *ROYAL BEDROOM*	
	CALVARY *DEATH, BURIAL, AND RESSURECTION*	
EL SHADDAI *THE ALL SUFFICIENT ONE*	**GIGAL** *CIRCUMCISION OF THE HEART*	**MIZPAH** *COVENANT OF GRACE THE CROSS MINISTRY*
HEBRON *WHOLE HEARTEDNESS WITH GOD*	**BETHESDA** *LORD OUR PHYSICIAN MIRACLES AND HEALING*	**SABOATH** *THE LORD OF HOST DELIVERANCE*
ZION *THE HOLY HILL WORSHIP AND PRAISE*	**RAPHA** *THE LORD OUR HEALER SPIRIT, SOUL, AND BODY*	**NEW JERUSALEM** *BRIDE OF CHRIST INTERCESSION*
	ADONAI *INTERCESSORS NEST*	
	SHAMMAH *THE LORD IS THERE PROPHET / INTERCESSION*	
	EL BETHEL SHILOH *HOUSE OF PRAYER KINDOM MINISTRY*	
	UPPER ROOM *HOLY GHOST FIRE*	
	INNER COURT *PRIEST'S PRAYER CLOSET*	

Each room has been named by God to depict the ministry He has established for that room. Details of that ministry are explained in a book in the room.

When one comes into the room, he/she enters into the prescence of the Lord. The Lord then meets that one at the point of his/her need, arresting one's fears or cares, if there be any.

† The *Sanctuary* is a center of a Priestly Prayer Body Ministry where saints co-labor with God night and day sending up priestly prayers for individuals, ministers, and ministries. Many come from far and near to be revived, healed, and join in the priestly ministry of prayer.

† The *Sanctuary* is also a Christian ministerial training center located in the quiet mid-western town of Whitewater, Wisconsin. Whitewater is 50 miles southwest of Milwaukee, 50 miles southeast of Madison and 100 miles northwest of Chicago.

† When one comes to the *Sanctuary* for overnight, he/she is placed in a room in which there is a special ministry. That one should seek to enter into the ministry of that room, therefore he/she should not bring outside material, i.e., tapes, books, etc., because what God wants that one to know or enter into is in the room already. What is in the room opens up the ministry of the room.

A brazen altar and burning bush grace each room.
**The Bush is
Still Burning.**

**The Lord says...
I Am That I Am.**

CPSIA information can be obtained at www.ICGtesting.com
Printed in the USA
LVOW070703280113

317459LV00001B/2/P